Biographies

Frida Kahlo

Painter of Strength

by Lissa Jones Johnston

Consultant:
Curt Germundson, PhD, Art History Professor
Minnesota State University, Mankato

Capstone press®

Mankato, Minnesota

Fact Finders is published by Capstone Press,
151 Good Counsel Drive, P.O. Box 669, Mankato, Minnesota 56002.
www.capstonepress.com

Library of Congress Cataloging-in-Publication Data
Johnston, Lissa Jones.
　　Frida Kahlo : painter of strength / by Lissa Johnston.
　　p. cm.—(Fact finders. Biographies. Great Hispanics)
　　Includes bibliographical references and index.
　　ISBN-13: 978-0-7368-6417-6 (hardcover)
　　ISBN-10: 0-7368-6417-2 (hardcover)
　　1. Kahlo, Frida—Juvenile literature. 2. Painters—Mexico—Biography—Juvenile
literature. I. Kahlo, Frida. II. Title. III. Series.
ND259.K33J64 2007
759.972—dc22　　　　　　　　　　　　　　　　　　　　　　　　　　2005037567

Summary: An introduction to the life of Frida Kahlo, the Mexican painter who
　　overcame polio and crippling pain to achieve world renown.

Editorial Credits
John Bliss and Jennifer Murtoff (Navta Associates), editors; Juliette Peters, set designer;
　　Jan Calek (Navta Associates), book designer; Wanda Winch, photo researcher/
　　photo editor

Photo Credits
Art Resource, NY/Schalkwijk, 10; The Bridgeman Art Library/Private Collection, Viva la Vida, 1954
(print), Kahlo, Frida (1910–54), 18; Corbis/Bettmann, 1; Courtesy of Banco de México, Fideicomiso
Diego Rivera y Frida Kahlo, 15, 17; Getty Images Inc./AFP/Emilie Sommer, 26; Getty Images Inc./
Topical Press Agency, 8; The Granger Collection, New York, 9, 13, 25; Image courtesy of Carolyn
Farb in memory of her son Jake Kenyon Shulman, 19; Photo by Nickolas Muray, (c) Nickolas Muray
Photo Archives, LLC, cover, 27; San Francisco Museum of Modern Art, Albert M. Bender Collection,
Gift of Albert M. Bender, 36.6061 Frida (Frieda) Kahlo, Frieda and Diego Rivera, 1931, oil on canvas,
39 3/8 in. x 31 in. (100.01 cm x 78.74 cm), Estate of Frieda Kahlo, Courtesy Banco de México, 5;
Throckmorton Fine Art, New York/Florence Arquina, 22; Throckmorton Fine Art, New York/Juan
Guzman, 23; Throckmorton Fine Art, New York/Guillermo Kahlo, 7; Throckmorton Fine Art, New
York/Victor Reyes, 14; Wikimedia/Peter Andersen, 21

Permission to reproduce works of art by Frida Kahlo for pages 5, 10–11, 15, 17, 18, and 19 is granted
by 2006 Banco de México Diego Rivera & Frida Kahlo Museums Trust, Ave. Cinco de Mayo No. 2,
Col. Centro, Del. Cuauhtemoc 06059, México D.F. Permission to reproduce works of art by Frida
Kahlo for pages 5, 10–11, 15, 17, 18, and 19 is also granted by el Instituto Nacional de Bellas Artes y
Literatura (INBA).

Table of Contents

Chapter 1

Young Talent

Frida Kahlo looked up at the large man on the platform, painting a **mural.** He was Diego Rivera, the most famous painter in Mexico. Did she dare disturb him? Gathering her courage, she asked him to climb down so they could talk.

Kahlo explained that her family needed money. She wanted to become an artist, but she wasn't sure if she had enough talent to actually sell any paintings. Kahlo had brought three of her paintings. She asked Rivera to look at them and give his opinion.

She turned each one around so that he could see them. Immediately, Rivera knew this young artist had talent. He told her that no matter what, she should never stop painting.

Kahlo painted this portrait of herself and Rivera in 1931.

Chapter 2

Childhood

Magdalena Carmen Frida Kahlo
y Calderón was born July 6, 1907, in
Coyoacán, Mexico. Everyone called
her Frida. Her father, Guillermo, was a
photographer. He took pictures for the
Mexican government. Her mother, Matilde
Calderón, was a housewife. She took care
of Frida and Frida's three sisters.

When she was six, Kahlo got **polio.** The
muscles in her right leg stopped working.
She had to stay home for nine months.

When Kahlo returned to school, her
right leg was thinner than her left leg.
She had a limp. She had to wear a shoe
with an extra-thick heel to help her walk.
Many children teased her.

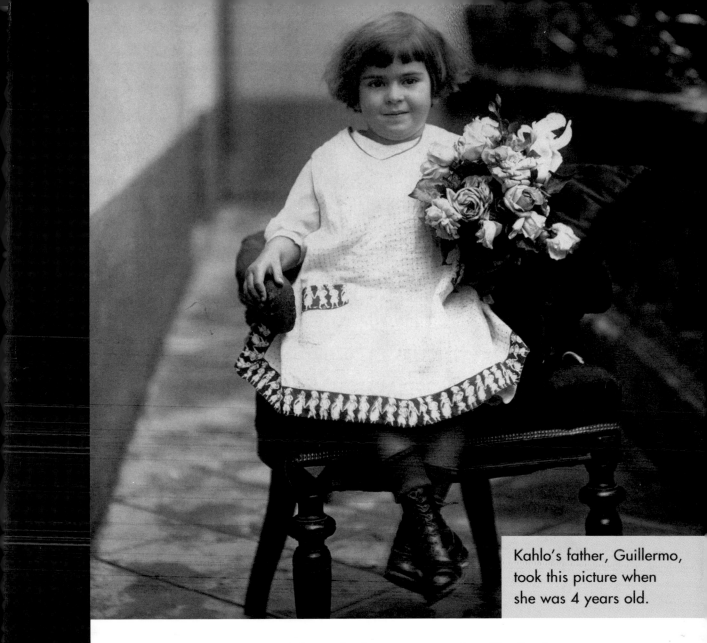

Kahlo's father, Guillermo, took this picture when she was 4 years old.

Kahlo's father wanted to help her get better. He took her to the park so she could play and get some exercise. Slowly, Kahlo's leg healed, and her limp disappeared. She returned to her playful ways.

The Revolution

When Kahlo was 3 years old, the Mexican Revolution began. People were angry with Mexico's government. The people wanted it to represent everyone, not just rich people. The people also wanted to be able to vote. Rebels fought government troops for ten years. Sometimes they fought in the streets outside the Kahlo house.

Kahlo grew up listening to her family discuss the revolution. She became interested in **politics** at an early age.

During the Mexican Revolution, soldiers and rebels fought in the streets. ▼

Kahlo had a playful spirit at an early age. In this portrait taken by her father, Kahlo (center) is dressed in a man's suit. ➡

School

Kahlo's mother taught her daughters how to cook, clean, and sew. She expected them to grow up, get married, and have children. Kahlo's father had other plans. He wanted Kahlo to attend the National Preparatory School in Mexico City. This was one of the best schools in Latin America. Kahlo enrolled at age 15.

The Accident

In 1925, during her senior year,
Kahlo was in an accident. A trolley
slammed into the city bus she was
riding. The trolley tore the bus apart.

▲ Kahlo painted *The Bus* in 1929, 4 years after her accident.

A piece of metal went completely through Kahlo's body. It broke her hip, leg, and some ribs. Her spine was broken in three places. People thought she was going to die.

Kahlo had so many broken bones that the doctors had to put her in a full-body cast. She was in a lot of pain and could move only her head. Kahlo was in the hospital for a month. When she returned home, she had to stay flat on her back for three more months.

Kahlo knew she had come close to dying. She was glad to be alive. Kahlo was determined to recover.

Chapter 3

Learning to Paint

A year after the accident, Kahlo's spine still had not healed properly. She had to wear plaster **corsets** and remain very still. She was bored.

One day she remembered the art supplies in her father's study. Kahlo knew very little about art when she began to paint. She had taken a few art classes. As she lay in bed, she painted and studied art.

Her parents had an easel made that fit over her bed. They also installed a mirror above the bed so that she could see herself while painting. Her first paintings were **portraits.**

By 1927, Kahlo was able to walk again. She got a job teaching art classes to children. Kahlo thought she might like to earn a living as an artist.

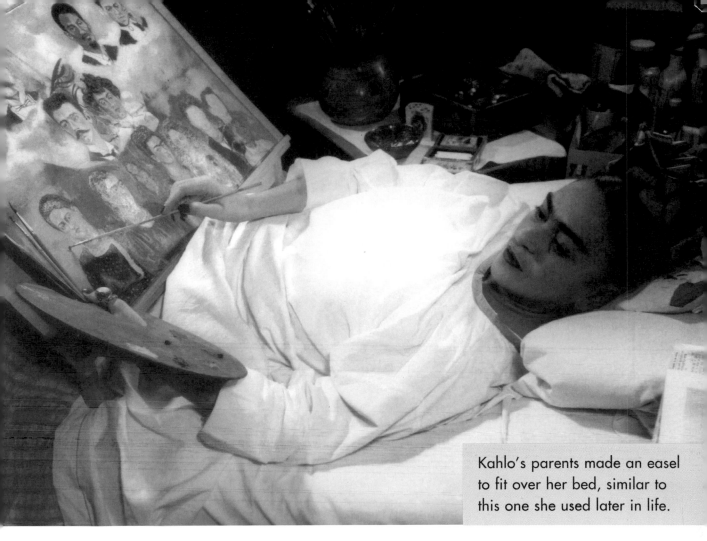

Kahlo's parents made an easel to fit over her bed, similar to this one she used later in life.

Kahlo made friends with many artists. They discussed the events of the day. One evening, Diego Rivera was present.

Kahlo remembered Rivera from her school days. He had painted a mural at her school. Kahlo visited him and showed him her work. Rivera was impressed.

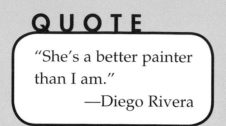

Rivera and Kahlo married in 1929. ▼

Although Rivera was much older than Kahlo, they shared many interests. Soon they fell in love. In 1929, they married. They made an unusual couple. Kahlo was small and delicate. Rivera was a huge man. Kahlo's father said they were like "an elephant and a dove."

Mrs. Diego Rivera

When Rivera received a **commission** in the United States, they moved to San Francisco. Rivera spent many hours away from home. Kahlo spent her time painting.

Kahlo and Rivera traveled often. The couple met many famous and wealthy people during their trips. Most people found Kahlo fun and exciting. They never would have guessed she had health problems.

Kahlo painted herself standing between Mexico, on the left, and the United States, on the right. ▼

Chapter 4

The Art World

After the couple returned to Mexico in 1933, Kahlo painted more often. Many of her paintings were self-portraits. In these, she faces straight ahead. Her eyebrows almost meet in the middle. Her dark hair might be pulled into a fancy style, worn loose, or cut short.

Kahlo used her paintings to show what she was feeling inside. When she felt sad, her paintings might show tears or a broken heart. She sometimes made paintings about her injuries. One painting shows her spine and how it was broken in the accident. People were used to seeing paintings of pretty flowers or bowls of fruit. They didn't know what to think of Kahlo's work.

QUOTE

"I paint myself because I am so often alone, because I am the subject I know best."
—Frida Kahlo

Kahlo also made paintings about her country and its people. Her art showed stark mountains, lush plants, and fruits bursting with color.

The University Gallery in Mexico City invited Kahlo to show her work there. People liked what they saw. In 1938, a gallery in New York City showed 25 of her paintings. Twelve of them sold. Kahlo was a success.

Kahlo's painting *Viva la vida* shows watermelons bursting with color. ➤

Surrealism combined the real world and the dream world, as shown in Kahlo's *The Little Deer*.

Surrealism

People in the art world said that Kahlo painted in a style called surrealism. This way of painting combined the real world and the dream world. Kahlo thought her paintings showed her real feelings, not her dreams.

In 1939, Kahlo was invited to show her work at an art show in Paris, France. The Louvre art museum bought one of her paintings. She was the first twentieth-century Mexican artist to have her work appear there.

Chapter 5

Return to Mexico

Kahlo's success in New York City and Paris did not continue in her personal life. When she returned to Mexico in 1939, she and Rivera were not getting along. Later that year they got a divorce. After the divorce, Kahlo made many paintings. Some people think they are her best work.

In 1940, an art show in Mexico City included some of Kahlo's work. A museum there bought one. Many people considered Kahlo one of the greatest artists in Mexico.

During 1940, Kahlo and Rivera decided to try to work out their problems. They remarried the same year. Kahlo was happy for a time. She painted as much as she could.

FACT!

Kahlo had many animals in her courtyard garden—a deer, turkeys, parrots, and dogs. A favorite pet was a small monkey named Fulang-Chang. His name means "any old monkey."

The Blue House is now a museum.

Kahlo decided to return to her family home in Coyoacán, Mexico. She remodeled the house to be more Mexican in style. She painted it in bright colors inside and out. It became known as the Blue House.

As Kahlo grew older, some of her old injuries bothered her more. Her back hurt if she worked too long. She often had to wear a plaster or leather corset to give her back support. The corsets were not comfortable, but they helped her back feel better.

A Wonderful Teacher

In 1943, Kahlo began to teach art for the Mexican Ministry of Education. She was a wonderful teacher, but, eventually, health problems forced her to stay home.

She did not want to stop teaching, so she invited her students to her home to continue their studies.

⬆ Kahlo often wore plaster corsets to help support her back. The corsets were often decorated.

FACT!

When Kahlo had to wear one of her many plaster corsets, she let people decorate it with paint and bright stickers. Some of her corsets are still on display at the museum in her former home.

Kahlo's health got worse in her later years. In 1950, she spent a year in the hospital as doctors tried to repair her back. The hospital staff loved her. While she was in the hospital, friends came to visit. Rivera rented a small room next to hers. Kahlo kept a positive attitude even when she was feeling her worst.

In the hospital, Kahlo kept up her spirits with puppet shows. ▼

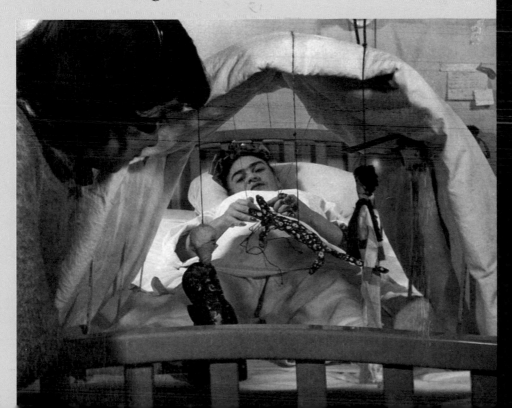

Chapter 6

Respected Artist

When Kahlo finally came home from the hospital, she could hardly walk. She would sit in a wheelchair or lie in bed to paint.

In 1953, Kahlo's work appeared in her first **solo** art show in Mexico. Her doctor gave her strict orders not to leave her bed. She obeyed his orders. Kahlo had a bed set up in the art gallery. She arrived by ambulance and was carried to the bed on a stretcher. The art gallery was filled with friends and fans. They were amazed to see her there.

In July 1954, Kahlo made her last public appearance at a political rally. A few days later, she died in her sleep. She was 47 years old.

Kahlo attended her solo art show in her bed. Her friends and fans surrounded her.

A Lasting Image

Kahlo created about 200 paintings during her lifetime. Artists study her. They respect the bold subjects and fine quality of her paintings.

Artists and fans alike are still inspired by her talent and strong will. Kahlo never let her pain keep her from living life to the fullest. She always remembered Rivera's advice. In a corset, in her wheelchair, or flat on her back, Kahlo never stopped painting.

Fast Facts

Full name: Magdalena Carmen Frida Kahlo y Calderón

Birth: July 6, 1907

Death: July 13, 1954

Parents: Guillermo Kahlo and Matilde Calderón

Siblings: three sisters, two half-sisters

Hometown: Coyoacán, Mexico

Husband: Diego Rivera

Major Works:
My Dress Hangs There (1933)
My Grandparents, My Parents, and I (1936)
The Two Fridas (1939)
Viva la vida (1954)

Time Line

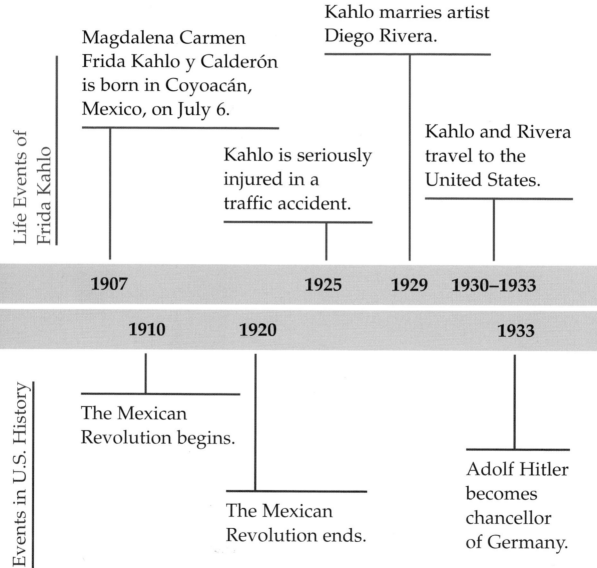

Life Events of Frida Kahlo

Magdalena Carmen Frida Kahlo y Calderón is born in Coyoacán, Mexico, on July 6.

Kahlo is seriously injured in a traffic accident.

Kahlo marries artist Diego Rivera.

Kahlo and Rivera travel to the United States.

1907   **1925**   **1929**   **1930–1933**

1910   **1920**   **1933**

Events in U.S. History

The Mexican Revolution begins.

The Mexican Revolution ends.

Adolf Hitler becomes chancellor of Germany.

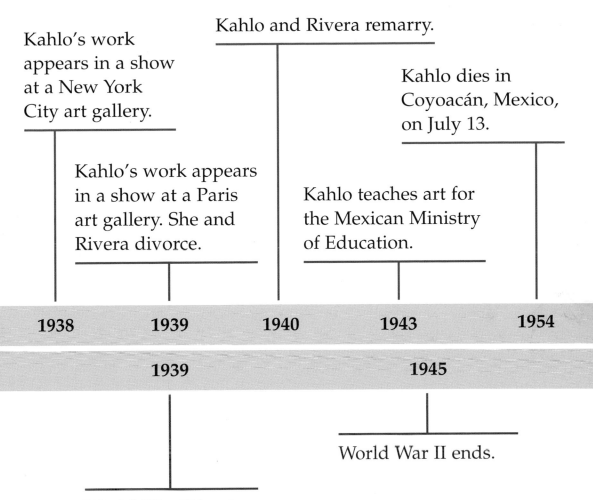

Kahlo's work appears in a show at a New York City art gallery.

Kahlo and Rivera remarry.

Kahlo dies in Coyoacán, Mexico, on July 13.

Kahlo's work appears in a show at a Paris art gallery. She and Rivera divorce.

Kahlo teaches art for the Mexican Ministry of Education.

1938   **1939**   **1940**   **1943**   **1954**

1939   **1945**

World War II begins.

World War II ends.

Glossary

commission (kuh-MISH-un)—money for work done

corset (KOR-set)—a woman's close-fitting, supporting undergarment

mural (MYU-ruhl)—a painting on a wall

polio (POH-lee-oh)—an infectious viral disease that attacks the brain and spinal cord

politics (POL-uh-tiks)—the debate and activity involved in governing a country

portrait (POR-trit)—a drawing, painting, or photograph of a person

solo (SOH-loh)—done by one person

surrealism (suh-REE-uh-li-zuhm)—a style of art in which scenes show ordinary objects in unusual or unexpected ways; sometimes described as "dreamlike."

Internet Sites

FactHound offers a safe, fun way to find Internet sites related to this book. All of the sites on FactHound have been researched by our staff.

Here's how:

1. Visit *www.facthound.com*

2. Choose your grade level.

3. Type in this book ID **0736864172** for age-appropriate sites. You may also browse subjects by clicking on letters, or by clicking on pictures and words.

4. Click on the **Fetch It** button.

FactHound will fetch the best sites for you!

Read More

Frith, Margaret. *Frida Kahlo: The Artist Who Painted Herself.* Smart about Art. New York: Grosset and Dunlap, 2003.

Laidlaw, Jill A. *Frida Kahlo.* Artists in Their Time. Danbury, Conn.: Franklin Watts, 2003.

Morrison, John. *Frida Kahlo.* The Great Hispanic Heritage. Philadelphia: Chelsea House Publishers, 2003.

Index